A WORD FROM THE LOKI

Maurice Riordan was born in Lisgoold, County Cork, in 1953. He was educated at University College, Cork – where he later taught – and at McMaster University in Canada. He lives in south London.

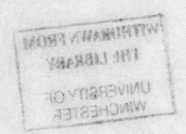

A Word from the Loki

MAURICE RIORDAN

faber and faber
LONDON · BOSTON

First published in 1995
by Faber and Faber Limited
3 Queen Square, London, WC1N 3AU

Photoset by Wilmaset Ltd, Wirral
Printed in England by Clays Ltd, St Ives plc

© Maurice Riordan, 1995

Maurice Riordan is hereby identified as author of this work
in accordance with Section 77 of the Copyright,
Designs and Patents Act 1988

A CIP record for this book is available from the British Library

ISBN 0 571 17364 0

2 4 6 8 10 9 7 5 3 1

for Niamh
and
for Michael

Acknowledgements

Thanks are due to the editors of the following publications in which some of these poems first appeared: *Irish Times, London Magazine, New Statesman and Society, Observer, Oxford Poetry, Pivot* (US), *Poetry London Newsletter, Poetry Review, Raven Introductions 4, Southern Review* (US), *Stet, Verse*. 'Milk' was a prizewinner in the 1992 National Poetry Competition. Eight of these poems were included in *Poetry Introduction 8* (Faber and Faber, 1993). I am grateful to the Arts Council/An Chomhairle Ealaíon and the Royal Literary Fund for their financial support.

Contents

The raw materials of utterance are drawn
from deep inside the body; impelled towards the mouth
where, first, they're cut and nimbly crafted by the tongue,
then given final shape by the contours of the lips;
after which, as words, they're imparted to the air.

LUCRETIUS

Time Out

Such is modern life   Stephen Dobyns

The two young ones fed, bathèd, zippered, read to and
     sung to. Asleep.
Time now to stretch on the sofa. Time for a cigarette.
When he realizes he's out. Clean out of smokes.
He grabs a fistful of coins, hesitates to listen before
Pulling the door softly to. Then sprints for the
     cornershop.

When he trips on a shoelace, head first into the path of a
     U-turning cab.
The screech of brakes is coterminous with his scream.
The Somalian shopkeeper, who summons the ambulance,
     knows the face,
But the name or address? No – just someone he
     remembers
Popping in, always with kids (this he doesn't say).

Casualty is at full stretch and the white thirtyish male,
Unshaven, with broken runners, is going nowhere. Is
     cleanly dead.
Around midnight an orderly rummages his pockets:
     £2.50 in change,
A latchkey, two chestnuts, one mitten, scraps of paper,
Some written on, but no wallet, cards, licence, or address
     book.

Around 2 a.m. he's put on ice, with a numbered tag.
Around 3 a.m. a child wakes, cries, then wails for
    attention.
But after ten minutes, unusually, goes back to sleep.
Unusually his twin sleeps on undisturbed till six o'clock,
When they both wake together, kicking, calling out *dada*,
    dada

Happily: well slept, still dry, crooning and pretend-
    reading in the half-light.
Then one slides to the floor, toddles to the master
    bedroom
And, seeing the empty (unmade) bed, toddles towards the
    stairs,
Now followed by the other, less stable, who stumbles
    halfway down
And both roll the last five steps to the bottom, screaming.

To be distracted by the post plopping onto the mat: all
    junk,
Therefore bulky, colourful, glossy, illicit. Time slips.
Nine o'clock: hungry, soiled, sensing oddness and
    absence,
Edgy together and whimpering now, when they discover
    the TV
Still on, its 17-channel console alive to their touch.

The Italian Parliament, sumo wrestling, the Austrian
    Grand Prix,
Opera, the Parcel Force ad, see them through to half past
    nine
When distress takes hold and the solid stereophonic
    screaming begins,
Relentless and shrill enough to penetrate the attention
Of the retired French pharmacist next door

Who at, say ten o'clock, pokes a broomstick through her
    rear window
To rattle theirs: magical silencing effect, lasting just so
    long
As it takes for the elderly woman to draw up her
    shopping list,
To retrieve two tenners from the ice-compartment, dead-
    lock her front doors,
Shake her head at the sunning milk, and make it to the
    bus.

Let us jump then to 10 p.m., to the nightmare
    dénouement . . .
No, let us duck right now out of this story, for such it is:
An idle, day-bed, Hitchcockian fantasy (though prompted
    by a news item,
A clockwork scenario: it was five days before that three-
    year-old
Was discovered beside the corpse of his Irish dad in
    Northolt).

Let us get *this* dad in and out of the shop, safely across
    the street,
Safely indoors again, less a couple of quid, plus the
    listings mags
And ten Silk Cut, back on board the sofa: reprieved,
    released, relaxed,
Thinking it's time for new sneakers, for a beard trim, for
    an overall
Rethink in the hair department. Time maybe to move on
    from the fags.

Shadows

I'm stretched on a grass bank looking for ladybirds,
God's cows as I know them, herding them with a straw
into my hand. Gently, so they won't fly off.
My father stops what he's at: scuffling mangolds
with an oblong stone, a hole at one end, hitched
to his first, diminutive, almost female tractor.
Stops, and stands on the headland to tell the time
by the fall of his shadow. Past midday: dinnertime.

Remembering, I feel hunger – or fear? An emptiness
above the groin. And I glance past the workbench
to where the children are playing by the sandbox,
an old bookcase whose shelves I've knocked out.
If I come to them now from behind, they'll look up,
surprised at how sombre and tall I must be.

Ghosts

I call it home: this house where I'm a guest,
in which the Sacred Heart illuminates
the bed, where still I sometimes wake in sweat,
where once I heard (but didn't see) a ghost.
My children, woken by the daws that roost
and squabble in the chimneys, come at dawn.
So I'm up, half-drugged but obliged to warm
and reassure. And quickly get them dressed.
It's question-and-answer hour, like do I
believe in Hell, was Joseph Jesus' dad?
And now, from my son: where did Grandpa die?
I tell him: right behind us, in my bed.
He looks — and I turn too, as though a sigh
must come from the warm clothes I've shed.

The Ladder

When a foal was born live my father stuck
the mess of clearings on a length of furze,
then draped them from a cross-beam in the shed,
away from cats and other scavengers.

Was this a sort of tally-stick, to keep
account of all the foals born in his day?
Or some pishogue observed against bad luck?
No one ever asked. My father didn't say;

yet each year added to the line of skins
along the beam, where now, like bats, they hang
above a combine – till some day the rafter gives
and they are thrown, uncounted, on the dung.

But they're still intact, obscured by spider-webs
and swallow droppings, of no consequence
to man or beast, feeding only the weevil
or whatever else is nourished in the silence.

I've poked a chance stick into the shed's gloom
and have, accidentally, dislodged the crust
of one: which hardly startles the shy foal,
curiously alive in morning frost

nor wakes my father's heart at such a moment
nor tells me who I am; yet I invent
a treacherous ladder and duly hang
the afterbirth where it seems to belong.

Rural Electrification 1956

We woke to the clink of crowbars
and the smell of creosote along the road.
Stripped to his britches, our pole-man
tossed up red dirt as we watched him
sink past his knees, past his navel:
Another day, he called out to us,
and I'll be through to Australia . . .
Later we brought him a whiskey bottle
tucked inside a Wellington sock and filled
with tea. He sat on the verge and told
of years in London, how he'd come home,
more fool, to share in the good times;
and went on to describe AC/DC, ohms,
insulation, potential difference,
so that the lights of Piccadilly
were swaying among the lamps of fuchsia,
before he disappeared into the earth.

Nickname

The windows of the Great House gave
onto a sloping lawn with avenue
that curved like some noble gesture –
up which Grandfather was trotting
his barouche in 1884-or-so,
when Lady Standish Barry cried out
'Oho, look at him – the young Buck
coming to have his rents reduced!'
And Standish had the first motor car
in County Cork, registered no. 1.
Joyriding from town that first day
he killed a sheep and pair of lambs,
but the next morning he was in
that passage there with three hoggets.
So said my father on Sunday morning
as he brushed and brushed his shoes,
blacked the night before, until they shone.

The Native

When 'Native' Flynn, after one too many,
gave his right arm to the teeth
of a spinning flywheel, the Navy staunched
the blood, sewed up the stump

and sent him back where he belonged –
on top of tractors, under combines
and dung-spreaders, searching for
elusive nozzles with a grease-gun.

He drank no more. Instead he took
to calling on the wives of farmers
after dark; but he never forgot
the rhythm of the licensed hours.

We'd hear him close to midnight
whistling past the graveyard,
where he'd raise an empty sleeve
in salute to his buried hand.

El Dorado

It was to be your first stroke
on the fair way to success –
the caravan we did up that spring
and towed the back road to Ballybunion.
You hadn't bargained for the lady dentist's
propriety about bed linen or the mess
could be left by a whirlwind weekend;
or the wagon train of depressions across
the weatherman's chart all of August.
So I became your solitary guest
and caretaker, guttling Agatha Christies
to the flutter of gaslight, my pallor
doubled in the rain-specked glass.
I uncovered a nest of drowned larks
on the fourth tee of the golf-course
and sat afternoons out on the rocks
to watch the sea coming, coming.

The Doctor's Stone

The Doc, in slippers and samite gown,
serves warmed milk and honey,
rashers, wads of blood pudding,
to cure a night on whiskey.
He's telling of a trip to Achill –
how, as he squatted on the sand,
he saw beyond the ocean's rim
the bright tips of a palm forest.
He never found the spot again
but knows he glimpsed Hy Brazil.
And he takes from a leather case
a stone, the size of a wren's egg,
that three days ago was lodged
inside his kidney. He traces
its passage to the bladder
down the urinary tract
into the palm of his hand.
Gives me the stone to hold.
It is so light and real
it could well be the one
I all but wrested from a dream.

An Egg

Off she treks on her own
up the path, between nettles,
to the tumbledown henhouse.
That houses nowadays
one hen and luckily,
this morning, one egg.

Which she's carrying cupped
before her, when a nettle
strays against her cheek.
Whereupon the egg slips
from her hold, opens and spills.
Changed as, now, her face is.

We say, it's only an egg.
There'll be more, we promise,
tomorrow, next day. Look,
here comes the hen! While she stands
pointing at the pieces
neither of us can mend.

England, his Love

At eleven he carried maps in his head
and became geographer to St Gobnait's.
The Iberian peninsula, Italy's ruffed boot,
tricky Denmark — materialized from his wrist
in chalk on the bare schoolroom floor.
The class, eight girls, stood far inland
while his hand shaped fjord and isthmus.
But it was England (Britain I should say)
that he loved — Scotland's ascetic front:
a head, just tilted back, listening,
then the long spine and solid rump
down to the flexed muscular leg . . .
He felt in it a form of nature
and perfected it: tense, marsupial England,
cocky little Wales sticking from her pocket.

Indian Summer

On the last afternoon
of my first visit

to London, I struck off
into the thick of Oxford Street,

where I bought, at Debenham's,
an imitation leopard-skin

suit (too tight) for my girlfriend
and a chocolate-brown

cord blazer (too large) for myself,
then turned the corner
,
onto the Edgware Road
to my ultimate destination,

Ann Summers' Sex Shop
(the original one, I believe)

where I bought an assortment
of condoms and a magazine

from the Lady herself,
who jingled her earrings

as she handed over
my purchases, saying

It must be gorgeous! Ireland,
the countryside, in this heat.

Lines to his New Instructress

Though I've an Olympic swimmer's chest,
hairlessly smooth and muscular, beware!

This is my poor repertoire of strokes,
a circumspect backfloat and a tense,

nose-down, breath-holding crawl to just
beyond my depth. Things I've mastered

despite mentors such as the Galway priest
who brought me at twelve/thirteen

to the ocean. I cannot tell you which
unnerved me more: the Latinized

sex-talk in the car, or the large hand
under my stomach, or that other time

when the only girl in sight lost half
her outfit to a wave. And he let me go,

either to absorb her cries, her squeals,
or drown – while he struck out from shore

on his vigorous, exemplary butterfly
between the arms of the bay.

Sandy's Lake

Above the townships Sandy offers me the map.
We're looking, he says, for somewhere beyond the reach
of vandals, pack-rats, lovers, collectors,
a place to moor the plane in the years ahead.
All morning we thread north through a necklace of lakes
and soon we lose the weekend cruisers and sea-doos,
at midday pass a lone white-water canoeist . . .
Yet each lake we come to is flawed: dirt track,
jetty, a floating dock; and one we chance on that's shaped
like a snow-pea, almost as green, too narrow for the map.
Sandy's eye measures take-off and landing distance
and we bring the plane down on her floats, cut the engine,
then wait for the noise to wash from our ears, long enough
to hear the water resettle against the shore.

Long Distance

So, for a season, he lived within
earshot of the railroads, in a room
furnished with sofabed, table, lamp,
silent fridge, a telephone.
At night he heard the freight trains
roll endlessly across the heartland.
They kept him up, sometimes till dawn,
beside a green radio and a map,
where he tracked the same baseball scores,
rapes, fires and murders, and much
the same humidity and heat
from the Lakes to the Gulf.
Once he dialled a number long distance.
Six, seven, eight times it rang.
No answer. He shifted the handset
to his chest, letting it ring and ring.

Flitcraft

When realtor Charlie Flitcraft broke for lunch
he had a deal simmering nicely on his desk,
a beautiful wife, two sons (whom he loved)
at home in the suburbs, a brand-new Packard,
and a golfing appointment that day at four.

The girder that smashed into the sidewalk
and bounced a splinter off his cheek
left him gazing ten, twelve floors up
at the unfinished shell of an office block.
He walked to the end of the street

and disappeared – just like that, like
a fist as you open your hand . . .
Or he would have but for a greenhorn dick
(who was really a writer with a block
as solid as the Chase Manhattan Bank)

who five, six years on in another town
played golf one afternoon with a man
who had a wife and baby (whom he loved),
a 1922 Packard, and a scar
you'd hardly notice across his right cheekbone.

Mandeville

Mid-morning, and a lone letter drifts onto the mat.

An invitation from a reputable, fringe theatre
to a sparkling new comedy. With shades of black.
To meet the author. To drink with the cast.
Addressed? Not to me – to Mandeville!
Mandeville, who skipped it years ago,
to squat in Notting Hill or Shepherd's Bush,
then coasted through the Med, on the African side,
to the East. Who, in each new town, headed
unerringly for the journalists' bar.
Who, by midnight, was locked in poker meltdown
with the purser of a ship bound for Queensland.
Leaving at daybreak. In need of a cook.
Mandeville – to whom the sun-dried tomato
was second-skin, who could elucidate the flavours
of Chambertin while telling just the right joke
to the hostess – I feared for you

out there on the hot belly of the globe,
halfway from New Zealand to Ecuador.
But nothing stopped you: not the forest, not the desert.
Not the screw-worm setting up shop next door
to your liver. Nor the Glasgow girl in Porto Algre
wanting your baby. Not the fevers, the nightmares.
And now you've re-entered our hemisphere
– that last card: two loons on a lake –
you'll touch down one of these nights in our lounge.
You'll demonstrate the side-kick to the throat
learned from that adept fräulein, Charlie Liu.
You'll show us the scar. And, since our kids
are school-age, we'll crack that quart of Wild Turkey,
matured eight years in charred oak and five more
in my cupboard. But *soon*, Mandeville, soon enough
to ponder this, from your one known correspondent.

And, Mandeville, we'll go to the play.

West 25th

for Sue

Another of those long weekends when kids
disappear, and a woman you might know
is raped on Main, or someone you don't scales
an office tower with a .22.
No wonder the freeways going North shimmer
and boil with traffic heading for the lakes.

Yet we're half-glad to be left to ourselves
in a suburban drowse, to wander up
a drive where only a video eye peers
into the glare; and we glimpse the better life
if a slice of perfect sky should one day drop
to make a swimming pool in our own backyard.

Night Drive

Slowed him down to an indecipherable slur
with rums and Coke, then mercifully blew him out
with a single high-velocity shot of bourbon
and parked him on the chesterfield at 4 a.m. . . .
only to find, less than an hour later, he has airlifted
to our bed where, bolt upright, he's telling his dream:
how they are back in Dublin, faced with a new
one-way system, but doing okay in Marcia's Pinto,
a steady forty along the quays, hitting each lights
at amber, Marcia at the wheel, the boys cheering them
   through,
no sweat, except she's driving in reverse.

A–Z

Afterwards she looked up the address
he'd given (on request) in her A–Z.
Honor Oak, Forest Hill: the names rang a bell.
Yes, she must have whizzed past them times.
Her finger traced the curve of his street.
Somewhere along there, she thought.
She worked out his route to the station,
to the library, to the High Street shops.
Cemeteries, several of them. Two parks.
In which had he made his morning run?

She looked again at the number he'd left,
with the proviso she wouldn't call.
Now she wanted to: not for his voice,
but for the background noises of the house,
for the stereo, the children, the dog,
the chitchat across the dinner table,
the tones of affection and reprimand.
She'd say, if he answered, just leave the phone
off the hook. She giggled, then quickly dialled.
But cut herself off at the first ring.

Apples

I climbed the apple tree in my friend's garden
and handed him down the fruit, which we carried
to the attic and arranged on newspaper
as a surprise for his wife. *Imagine,*
he said, *the smell when she comes home . . .*
a month from then, and a month since
we'd seen her off, with their infant, at the airport –
on the same evening I'd run into you
on the street and, though there were reasons
(still best kept to ourselves) we shouldn't have,
we went for a drink and afterwards drove
to the country and parked the car in the rain.
I don't know how well my friend's plan worked
or how much it meant to you, that night
years ago, or if you ever think of it now.
All I can say is there were mirrors in the attic
and the last thing I did before shutting the door
was to angle them, so that I could see
the apples travelling out from the room.

Fish

Okay, not the defrosted Sole Florentine
you served the first time you had me around,
nor the oysters, drained from a jar and tossed
with linguine, I rustled up in return.
But what of the scallops bought fresh in Cork,
cautiously nicked of their coral and splashed
with Sancerre, when we had money.
What of our weekly raids on the fish stalls
of Barcelona, for *merluza* (whatever it was),
our ventures with squid, with quenelles
of pike, with pomfret, red mullet, lophius.
And that night on the way from Tarragona
when, our gums watering for the turmeric
and garlic, we bolted a roadside paella.
The light changed to lemon across the bay,
remember, and we stumbled home (home! a
hammock-shaped bed eight stone flights up
in the *barrio gotico*) singing rounds . . .

So, we slackened off. But still for birthdays,
for anniversaries, or on a whim, I'd bring home
something from Soper's or from Brewer Street,
and get to work while the babies slept.
If they slept. Scaling, filleting, boning,
absorbed in the smells: fresh, cooked, stale.
We might get somewhere again, I thought, with luck

and persistence. Think of the silky salmon mousse,
the peppery clout of my *bisque Normandie*!
Latterly my tastes veered oriental: saffron,
lemon grass, the cool transparencies of Japan . . .
But now what can I do: when, after ten years,
you announce that, truly, you detest fish.

Steak

Just when she thought all that was finished,
it hits her again out of the blue,
slips from her tongue like a swear-word: steak.
And she's gone, not to some wiseacre butcher
who'll fob her off with smiles and a T-bone.
To the supermarkets, where she's free to pinch
and poke, to sniff if need be. And she finds it
at Waitrose (as it happens): a half-pounder,
beautifully marbled and plum-coloured,
reduced to half-price. How that makes her laugh!

(This isn't some 90s anchorite, but one who knows
the business of old: Augustine on his day off.)

Now she is home and, good, they are still out.
She opens the backdoor, windows, the wine.   ·
She reddens the pan, takes the meat to warm
between her palms, then slaps it on . . .
Two minutes a side: but hot, hot, hot.
She waives the mushrooms and the onions, just
a tittle of garlic, seasonings, claret.
Does she tremble somewhat? Never mind,
no fat or gristle to speak of. She sits
in the afterglow, dandles her wine, burps.

The Cactus Garden

Schnapps, a spiked fondue, more schnapps

— almost enough that drizzling Christmas Eve
to explain why, at the Elephant and Castle,
he jumped the train, leaving wife and kids
to gape at his exit from their lives.
Only to go on by bus, but miss his stop,
the street where he banked and shopped,
the park where day by day he strolled,
till he found himself at the end of the route.

He walked back the unfamiliar streets,
his first landmark a cactus garden
(last seen in August when one thin saguaro
was in flower) encased now in a homemade
pagoda of glass that shed in the rain,
under the mercury light, a moonish gleam.

Last Call

Home late, his house asleep, a man goes to the phone,
and from habit, expecting nothing, touches the Recall.
But this time he tenses to hear the electronic scramble,
the pause before the lottery digits fall into place.
At the other end, sure enough, he hears a male voice,
no one he recognizes, repeating *Hello, hello?*
He can hear background piano, Chopin or John Field,
establishing a room, smoke-filled, larger than his,
where wine in a discarded glass is losing its chill,
while the voice continues, good-humoured, persuasive:
Come on, say something. He tries to picture a face, a hand,
to fit the voice, still in his ear, still going on, *Last chance* . . .
He hangs up, his own hand shaking with intimacy.

Milk

This notebook in which he used to sketch
has, on its expensive-looking black cover,

a sprinkle of whitish stains: of the sort
sure to detain the unborn biographer.

Could they be the miniaturist's impression
of the northern sky, his Starry Night?

Or might lab-tests point to something else?
That they are, in fact, human milk-stains,

the effect of lactic acid on cheap skin,
and date from five years earlier —

a time when his wife's hyperactive glands
used to lob milk right across the room

to the wing-chair in which he dozed,
the sketchbook (it seems) closed in his hands.

Though he felt its light lash on his skin
many a night, he never took to that milk

and wished only for a wider room.
A failure of imagination, you might claim,

though it could be he needed more
of human kindness from that source then.

You could even say that the milk stopped,
but the acid didn't. That he replied in kind.

And thus it began: the pointless unstoppable game
across a room, in which a child grew

less small, and became the mesmerized umpire
looking now one way, now the other.

Topiary

A year ago the weather was better.
By now the almond blossom had come and gone.
Basil covered the sill, ready to grace
salads of shallots and beef tomatoes.
We had been to the country; had seen sheep
with their lambs, peacocks; had ushered
the children around Penshurst, up and down
the staircases and out onto the lawns;
we had learned a new word: topiary.
And one morning we put on sunglasses,
drew deeply from our joint account
and presented ourselves at Homebase.
We loaded the van with pots of juniper,
a barbecue, coals, and garden furniture.
There was to be no end of corn-on-the-cob,
seafood kebabs, and Australian Chardonnay.
This is no dream, no shrill inventory
of the housebound and vindictive mate.
From where I stand, I can see the rain
hitting the round weatherproof tabletop,
holding off, then hitting it again.

The Table

Remember that table we used to want?
That we agreed should be plain, serviceable wood,
with drop leaves, to complete our tiny room.

Something to which baby-chairs could be yoked,
that might expand, in time, for supper-parties,
for renewed experiments with the spirit lamp.

Across which, over the wine and profiteroles,
we could tell each other stories: how I was thrown
off a buckrake under the back wheel of the tractor;

while you, a girl in Ontario, stuck your barrette
in a socket and were saved from electrocution
by its rubber band. You'd gloss *barrette* as hair-slide.

And we'd agree these were simultaneous events,
so we might chuckle once more at the providence
of coming together, to increase and multiply,

here, around a table we'd hunted down in New Cross,
having perambulated your bump (the twin-tub!)
through loft upon loft of displaced furniture.

We never gave up on that table, you know,
not officially. And I've kept an eye out for it,
scanning from habit the small ads and auction lists.

Would you believe me now if I telephoned
to say I'd found one? Nothing fancy or antique,
but an honest specimen of forties joinery.

It would require work. That marbled green veneer
would have to go, along with several nicks
and gouges, obscure stains, other people's memories.

Sure – a lot of work. But you can still see
somewhere inside it the original shining deal,
the plain altar still fit for household ceremonies.

Chair

At the local museum of Natural History
they used to keep, half-way up the stairs
that now are part of its Living World exhibit,
an iron chair. Sixteenth-century Spanish,
a remnant of the Inquisition – crudely forged
but sculptural, less a chair than a study
of the body's lightweight engineering.

It had bracelets for the wrists and ankles,
bracts to disengage the trunk and thighs,
an armature – with chin-rest – to hold the head,
pressure-points at forehead, temples, jaw.
It seemed designed to relax the occupant,
to neutralize perfectly the vertical
and active musculature of the human frame.

The emphasis on the skull, on bone, assumed
proportion once one saw how it elided
the softer organs, the surfaces of pleasure
or cruelty; that, tacitly, it enforced
an ambience both reasonable and intimate;
that the isolation of the mouth and ear
ensured the pure exchange of intelligence.

Thus provided, the seasoned interrogator
need never lose his patience, had little cause
to raise his voice, or hand, when he made
fractional adjustments to the screws.
As for the sitter: he must learn the virtue
of minimal fuss, to restrain impulse,
to cut irrelevance from the process.

Here sat mad, devious, or saintly fools,
the merely dreaming. And were measured.
Here the wayward, fantasticated imaginings
of an age shrunk to their few essentials,
were calibrated in terms of stillness, pain,
the resistance of bone. Here, if any place,
the brain found the eccentric force

to maintain the integrity of its visions.

Beds

the mattressphere   Les Murray

What's surprising is the uniformity
of their elevation from the floor.
They hit me just above the knee,
a few inches higher than a chair-seat,
lower than a consultant's couch.
Given our range of height, or length –
Philippinos, Inuit, Icelanders –
this has little to do with ease
in slipping in and out of them.
For convenient use, or frolics,
one could find better paradigms:
rush-strewn floors, tree-strung hammocks,
military bunks and cabin berths.
Yet those have the air of novelty,
of camp, adventure stories, sex:
the realtors of Anchorage and Perth,
Holiday Inns to the east and west,
aren't laying them on. Unlike
bath-tubs, or even fireside chairs,
there's little eccentricity of choice:
few ovals or L-shapes; no rockers!
The uniformity *is* surprising.

Can it have to do with parents
bending over us, with children
arriving in the dark? Is it something
pre-verbal, an element in ur-grammar,
that articulates *safety* where we feel
we're most at risk, *comfort*
when tending, or being tended to?
Or is it somehow more abstract,
a mathematical law, Platonic
but unformulated, one we've hit upon
by trial and error, and which now
we're holding on to – whereby each night,
surrendering to solitude and dream,
we align our bodies with the earth,
yet desire a specific elevation.
Most nights we climb aboard,
curl up, never think about it.
Once or twice we'll stand beside one
beseeching somebody not to leave us,
not to die or fail to love us,
not tonight. Or else we'll fall in prayer
to its emptiness, whatever god it holds.

L. S. Lowry's *Man Lying on a Wall*

after Michael Longley

I'm asleep, you say, possibly dead.
I sleep then with my mouth closed
on a cigarette, with one eye open
to watch its delicate tower of ash.
That explains the stiff expression,
though not the pink buttonhole
or squashed bowler, blue cravat,
the suggestive spire my hands make,
the size fourteen shoes – nor the fact
I've one foot stretched on cool brick,
the other in perspective's mid-air . . .

Have another look at these bricks:
no two are the exact same shape
or shade of municipal brown.
Each one was drawn, or laid,
so you can see how the wall rose,
level and true, to carry me off
(a tramp or executive?) halfway
from pavement to the sky,
while you edge closer in the queue.

The Check-up – June 1992

God, coming back from his tour of the galaxies,
decides to drop in on Earth. At first
he cannot pinpoint its whereabouts. Then he remembers
the exquisite colouring. So much smaller, it looks,
now he's no longer involved with the details.
Still it's a beaut, and in its prime – good,
he reckons, for a few more billion years.
He turns it round, to admire the elegance
of design. And once again, now justly proud
of the balance, patience, sense of humour,
the fluidity and tact of the execution.

He gives it the routine check-up. Temperature?
A little high, though nothing to worry over.
Some evidence of polar wobble but self-correcting.
He graphs the trajectories of the 70-odd asteroids
that will, from time to time, cut across its path.
Briskly, he redoes those ticker-tape sums,
while popping questions about geological ache,
species count, toxin distribution, who's President.
He does a comprehensive, in-depth brain scan –
but not the Veep's, ha-ha. Finds all is in order,
nothing untoward or original. Normal development.

He folds his instruments, decides on a friendly chat.
He loves to catch up on the gossip: the current craze
in particle theory or installation sculpture,
what Ms Bordes is up to these days, the latest in
bar-slang, cyberpunk, Kerry jokes. That sort of stuff.
It is then he happens on a detail, something slight
– but unprecedented, unforeseen – that wipes the smile
clean from his face. He flushes with impotent rage,
for there is nothing, nothing at all that he can do.
Sweet Jesus, he seems to mutter, as he hurries
away, looking suddenly old and frail.

The Real Thing

We live inside a steady atomic bombardment
where everything emits corpuscular streams of images
and so conveys colours, shapes and noises to the senses
– according to the unified theory of Lucretius
who killed himself, we're told by Saint Jerome, when sickened
by a love draught, by love gone wrong, so to speak,
in its chemical form; having by then composed,
during the catastrophic last years of the republic,
De Rerum Natura, the nature of things or simply Nature:
which we know sensationally, first-hand, through the body.
Jerome, as you'd expect, approved the Roman's assaults
on pagan gods, as well as his most un-Roman-like
recoil from sexual love: so the poem found passage,
in one defective manuscript, into modern hands;

where it arrives still fresh with that heady first draught
of Attic speculation, as yet unhindered by results.
Nothing is beyond its range: the particles of matter,
magnets, dreams, physiology, earthquake, British weather,
the temperaments of the wild beasts and 'military use
    thereof' . . .
It enquires into questions such as how it is we hear,
though we cannot see, people talking in the room next door;
why, as we bend towards a looking-glass, we see ourselves
rise from its depths. These are not 'thorny' questions,
Lucretius assures us: though lacking (as he must) the law
of incidence and reflection, and impossibly far
from any inkling of frequency or amplitude,
his hypotheses have here the demonic gleam of de Selby
with something of a small boy's ingenuity and charm.

But on the phenomena themselves he is vivid
and exact: we see the woodcutter on a far-off hill
raise the axe to shoulder level, even as its report
reaches the ear; shadows walk beside us in the moonlight;
we bend above a puddle that reflects the heavens;
those heavens open and discharge their hail; the air splits
and we smell – as we never have in life – the alien,
sulphurous stench of a house gutted by a lightning bolt.
Or he can be sweet. Then the stiff hexameter swells
with brave notions, gentle expressions: the pear-tree
gathers through its whole gnarled form the essence
of the pear and presents its flesh to the appetite;
cows roll in pasture, heavy with milk oozing from their dugs
('undiluted milk', he writes, to make the sucklings 'tipsy').

Here then is nature's peaceful traffic: Mars lies asleep
in Venus' lap absorbing her moist, maternal atoms . . .
Yet when he speaks of human love, it is 'incisions',
'stings' and 'loss of strength'. Even as the eye is drawn
to the radiant, volatile surfaces of girls or youths,
we're warned off; and when the symptoms mount from cuts
and bruises to inflammation, delirium, unquenchable fire,
we're told 'distract yourselves with substitutes'
or else: *Sleep alone* – by this bewildered epicure
(deranged, the Fathers claim, from an overdose of potion)
who, in refrain, recollects his childhood home, the nights
he lay awake watchful of the Etruscan images
and having dreamt, perhaps, of Iphigenia;
a bookish, high-strung boy frightened by the gods

who would complete a lifetime's scientific effort,
not with ebullient strophes to Venus or Apollo,
but with the Plague of Athens, 430 BC
– in this to prove himself fit for mortal combat,
the poet of the vulnerable body: when the atomic cloud,
wind-borne off Egypt's salty marshes, invades the throats
of the citizens; carrying the weapons of cold and heat;
imposing a regime of thirst and hunger; which attacks
the citadels of life, whose seat – located in the breast –
totters but still holds; exquisite instruments are brought
to bear; and no relief, except in prayers and outcries.
Then not even those; the lively atoms have found
the tongue, 'interpreter of the mind', and disconnected it.
Nothing now but unutterable pains. And so it ends.

Some Sporting Motifs

The ball-games of the north-western tribes
have their origins in the spoils of war.
The ball at your feet *is* the trophy,
the head of the enemy you have slain
being booted homewards through the fields
or passed along the line of warriors,
after the glorious summer campaign.

As for games with sticks – such as shinty,
hurling, hockey, golf – you must compare
the design of the modern cricket-ball
with its analogue, the Irish *sliotar*:
two 'eights' of dried skin, hemp-sewn around
a light, bouncey core. *Balls* it could be called,
or *bollocks*, to indicate its dual number;

while the stick itself is a surrogate,
toy sword – for this was the pastime
of the camp-followers: the boys and women.
Hence, the spectacle of camogie.
Hence, indeed, the sphere of harness leather
patched around a core of whiskey corks,
sewn and re-sewn, by my mother.

A Word from the Loki

The Loki tongue does not lend itself
to description along classical lines.
Consider the vowels: there are just four,
including one produced by inspiration
(i.e. indrawn breath), which then requires
an acrobatic feat of projection
to engage with its troupe of consonants.
The skilled linguist can manage, at best,
a sort of tattoo; whereas the Loki
form sounds of balletic exactness.
Consider further: that the tribe has evolved
this strenuous means of articulation
for one word, a defective verb
used in one mood only, the optative.

No semantic equivalent can be found
in English, nor within Indo-European.
Loosely, the word might be glossed as *to joke*,
provided we cite several other usages,
such as *to recover from snakebite*;
to eat fish with the ancestors;
*to die at home in the village, survived
by all of one's sons and grandsons*.
It is prohibited in daily speech,
and the Loki, a moderate people
who abjure physical punishments,
are severe in enforcing this taboo,
since all offenders, of whatever age
or status, are handed over to *mouri*

– sent, in effect, to a gruesome death:
for the victim is put on board a raft,
given a gourd of drinking water, a knife,
and one of those raucous owl-faced
monkeys as companion, then towed
to midstream and set loose on the current.
Yet the taboo is relaxed at so-called
'joke parties': impromptu celebrations
that can be provoked by multiple births
or by an out-of-season catch of bluefish.
They are occasions for story-telling
and poetry, and serve a useful end
in allowing the young to learn this verb
and to perfect its exact delivery.

For the word is held to have come down
from the ancestral gods, to be their one gift.
And its occult use is specific: to ward off
the Loordhu, a cannibalistic horde,
believed to roam the interior forest,
who are reputed to like their meat
fresh and raw, to keep children in lieu of pigs,
and to treat eye and tongue as delicacies.
The proximity of danger is heralded
by a despondency that seems to strike
without visible cause but which effects
a swift change among a people by nature
brave and practical, bringing to a stop
in a matter of hours all work, play, talk.

At such crises, the villagers advance
to the riverbank and, as night falls,
they climb into the trees, there to recite
this verb throughout the hours of darkness.
But since, in the memory of the village,
the Loordhu have never yet attacked,
one has reason to doubt the existence
of an imminent threat to the Loki –
who nonetheless continue, in suspense, their chant.
At once wistful and eerie, it produces
this observable result: that it quells
the commotion of the guenon monkeys
and lulls, within its range, the great forest.